CW01455403

THE PARISH OF ST. GENNYS

A PICTORIAL HISTORY
1900 - 2000 AD.

THE LIFE AND TIMES OF A
NORTH CORNWALL
COMMUNITY AND ITS PEOPLE

St. Gennys Gazette

2000 A.D.

This logo was designed by Andrew Bird and adopted in 1988.

Published by the St Gennys Gazette
Crackington Haven
Cornwall. EX23 0JJ
United Kingdom

First Published 2000 AD.

Copyright © 2000 The St Gennys Gazette
All Rights Reserved

ISBN: 0 9536919 O X

AWARDS
FOR ALL

Printed in the United Kingdom by St Gennys Gazette
Binding by Plymouth City Council Bookbinding Department
Covers by Palace Printers, Lostwithiel

PREFACE

It is from their history that villages, like countries, derive their characters, ideals and sense of community.

The end of the 20th Century may be a good time for looking back over the past hundred years at those people and their activities whose lives produced what we now enjoy.

The history of a nation shows the great sweep of events which determined its rise or fall, but beneath such grand forces lies the true foundation of small communities living each day, every one unique in some way, and marked by their struggles and triumphs, progress or decline, joys and grief.

St.Gennys Parish has roots beyond the mists of time. Established by Celtic missionaries on the windswept, romantic Cornish coast, with cliffs, beaches, and coombes, it has offered a salubrious haven for both native Cornish and eager immigrant. The diversity of its inhabitants, their talents, skills and achievements over the years, has produced a robust and lively community. Fortunately, the art of photography lets us see how our predecessors lived, the institutions they founded, their entertainments and celebrations, and their adaptations to the social and technological changes of this century.

When the St.Gennys Gazette canvassed possible interest in a pictorial history, response was overwhelming. Family albums, postcards, snapshots and memorabilia were retrieved from attics, cupboards and boxes, their owners accompanying delivery by vivid recollections of the people, their families and groups, and views of the Parish, long since changed. Such widespread enthusiasm was so heartening that the Gazette staff resolved to produce this Pictorial History.

Compilation, editing, printing and collating were all done on a volunteer basis. While assistance was given by many, many people, particular appreciation is due to the Parish Council and Awards for All, who underwrote the purchase of supplies; to Chris Berry, whose computer skills enhanced all the pictures and produced the printing plates; to Leonard Ward whose vast knowledge of village history was indispensible, to Adrian Abbott for collating, and collecting of material from many sources, far and wide; and to Henry Boettinger and Chris for the printing. Regretfully, we cannot list all those whose comments, ideas and suggestions we were privileged to receive. Any such list would be both incomplete and a long one indeed.

Shirley Boettinger, Editor

DEDICATION

This book is dedicated to every child of the Parish who received a free copy, and who will, hopefully, <u>date</u> and <u>identify</u> their photographs for the next Millennium!

Foreword

While St.Gennys Parish has many features similar to other rural communities, it is also unique.

Nestling on the rugged Atlantic Coast of North Cornwall, laced by ancient hedges, carved by its streams, and graced by buildings of all vintages, it is recorded in the Domesday Book, and been inhabited for centuries before that.

The history of St.Gennys mirrors the history of Britain. Monks, farmers, fishermen, miners, craftsmen, musicians, church and chapels, teachers, schools, shops, clubs and pubs have all contributed over the years and evolved to produce today's lively village life.

This book aims to capture the spirit of an idyllic place through photographs of the people, activities and events of the last hundred years. All pictures have come from present and former residents whose trust and support made it possible. Their enthusiastic motivation springs from a gratitude to those who came before us, and a desire to record our heritage for future generations.

Since boyhood, a passion for knowledge of Cornwall in general, and St.Gennys in particular, gave me a rewarding awareness of our rich history and its colourful characters.

It is my fervent wish that this volume may likewise enkindle in our youngsters an appreciation for their roots which will give them as much pleasure as I have enjoyed from such discovery.

Leonard B. Ward

CONTENTS

*"The best thing which we derive from history
is the enthusiasm that it raises in us."*
Goethe

1900 - 1910

The Wedding Couple: Henry Knight and Ethel Edwards with Mabel and 'Granfer' Edwards at the Old Cottage, (near the present village shop).

..........and, 'going away' after the wedding.

Albert Cory.

The blacksmith at Mineshop.

Henry Knight.

Local carpenter for many years, whose apprentices included Boxer Sandercock and Fred Bird.

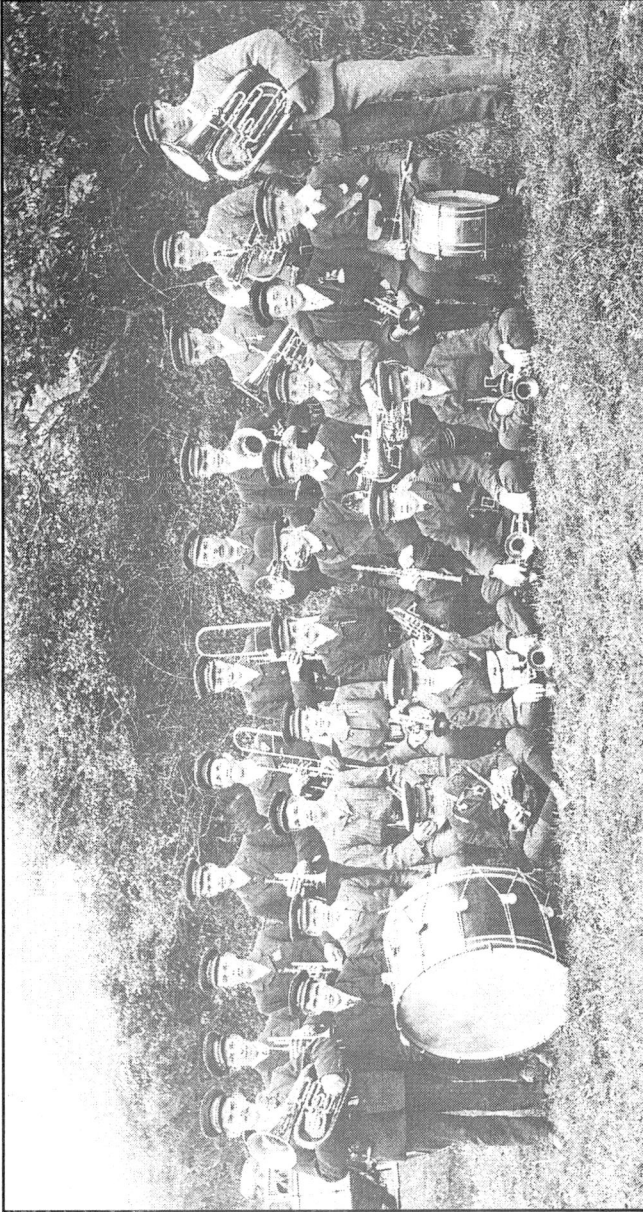

Back Row: Rocky Smeeth, Ewart Gliddon,John Hazel,Mark Wickett,Claude Sandercock,Harold Patten, J.H. Goodman, Edward Heal,Charles Heal, W. Tilley.

2nd Row: E. Gliddon,P. Heal,Ambrose Sandercock,Tom Ward,Henwood Cowling,Bandmaster Cook, C. Cowling,Cecil Heal,E. Brookham,Bryant Heal.

Front Row: Edgar Ward,Ernest Sandercock,Alfred Ward,Tom Sandercock

Uncle William, Aunt Dorothy, Donald, Ellen and Claude Sandercock at 'Rosecare'.

Mr W.J. Sandercock and Clarence outside the grocer's shop at Sweets.

Claude Sandercock's mother and father outside the general store at Rosecare in 1900.

Red Devons
grazing on Penkenna.
Notice the absence of
buildings on Millball.

The Haven through to
Dogshouse.

Bea Ponson, Maude, Flo and Edith Parnall with Edith White, Muriel Hay and
Nancy Huxham at the beach hut in 1907.

The mine captain's house at Mineshop.

Cleave Farm, St Gennys circa 1900.

Collecting seaweed from the beach.

Mary Stacey on the Clapper Bridge.

St Gennys School in 1905.

St. Gennys' Coronation Festivities.

1902

PRESENTED TO

Mary Grace Sandercock

Edward the Seventh

by the Grace of God, of the United Kingdom of Great Britain and Ireland, and of the British Dominions beyond the Seas King, Defender of the Faith, Emperor of India.

Born November 9th 1841.

Succeeded to the Throne, January 22nd 1901.

Crowned, 9th August, 1902.

"GOD SAVE THE KING"

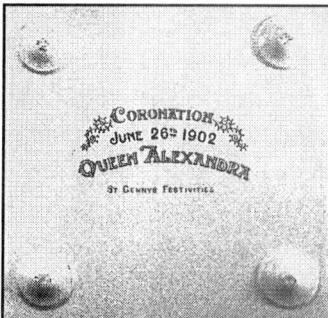

CORONATION
JUNE 26th 1902
QUEEN ALEXANDRA
St Gennys Festivities

Memorablia from the Coronation of Edward VIIth and Queen Alexandra, 1902. The certificate was presented to Mary Grace Sandercock. The discrepancy in the two Coronation dates is due to the fact that the Coronation was *planned* for June 26th 1902, but was *postponed*, until August 9th, due to the King's illness.

Band practice at Mineshop early in the century.

Elizabeth Cory (left) with friend.

Greta Cory Coombes with 'Teddy', later Mrs A.R. Anthony, then Mrs F.W. Skinnard. Probably taken at Rosecare.

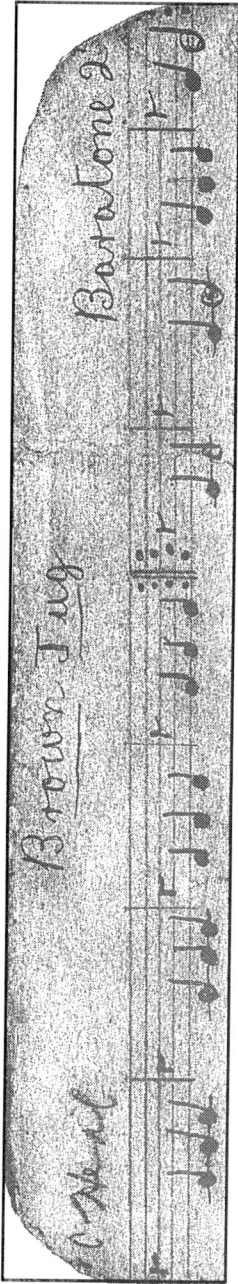

ONE OF THE FIRST PIECES THE BAND PLAYED

Mr & Mrs Boney, with Will and Dot at Pencuke.

A family outing leaves Rosecare.

Mr L. Appleton and the Rev. J. Thompson, Vicar of St Gennys 1898-1902.

The Rev. W.H. Browne, Vicar of St Gennys from 1902-1917.
When the Band practised in the schoolroom, he complained of the noise during his services. The problem was resolved by the Band changing their practice night from Wednesday to Saturday, during Lent.

John Hocking Goodman who shared the first secretaryship of the Band with William Jenkins.

Fencing at 'White Lodge' and..............

Thatching at 'White Lodge'.

Teas at
'Little Penn'.

Mr.& Mrs Beacon, teachers at St Gennys School in the 1900s.

Mrs Goodman and Lois ready for church.

Granfer Goodman & son.

Run aground! A group taken on the beach on August Bank Holiday, 1900, including Donald Sandercock, Winnie Heal, Georgina Cory, Alberta Shepherd, Uncle John Sandercock, Bertha Cowling and Polly Rich.

The wedding of Mr & Mrs W. Jenkins taken at Mineshop, 1906. Group incudes Albert Cory, Laura Goodman, Enoch Heal Winnie Heal, Lois Goodman, Lady Harris, Will Jenkins, Alice Cory, and Kate Marshall.

Congdons.

A shooting party at 'Higher Tresmorn' with Will Jenkins on the far right.

16

Dorothy and Jack Dingley on the beach in 1904.

WAINHOUSE CORNER,

A jingle approaching Wainhouse Corner.

Two different views of St Gregory's Chapel in St Gennys Church.

ST. GREGORY'S CHAPEL, ST. GENNY'S CHURCH

The earlier one shows the window behind the altar, and the later, the picture which now hangs in the North Aisle.

Brockhill Sunday School Tea Treat at Ludon.

Ludon Farm with Penkenna beyond.

Bastard Mill near Treworgie.

Granfer Rogers of 'Trevigue', on the footpath at Strangles, taken from a postcard produced to advertise the newly opened Southern Railway from Waterloo to Padstow.

St. Genny's Church

The copper canopy on St Gennys Church was added in the early 1900's, but the Cornish gales soon removed it.

Another early view of the Haven.

Mr J.J. Smeeth with Rocky, William, a friend + a dog at Tresmorn.

Flanders
House

and

Flanders Cottage
with Edith Parnall
up the ladder.

1911 - 1920

THE GREAT WAR,
1914—1919.

The following is a list of the Men who served from the Parish of ST. GENNYS :—

FALLEN.

Lance-Corporal WILLIAM RUSH, 1st D.C.L.I.
Private ALFRED MARSHALL WARD, Wiltshire Regiment.
Private CLIFFORD HOCKIN, Duke of Cornwall Light Infantry.
Private MARK WICKETT, 2nd Royal Irish Regiment.
Private WILLIAM COTTELL, 2nd D.C.L.I.
Private CHARLES M. LUXON, 2nd Canad'ans.
Private SYDNEY DYMOND, 2/4 D.C.L.I.
Private FRANK GLIDDON, Hants Regiment.

RETURNED.

Sergeant W. JENKINS, 21st Siege Battery, Ammun. Col'mn.
Driver FREDERIC MARTIN, D.C.L.I.
Driver CHARLES COWLING HEAL, R.A.S.C.
Gunner FRANCIS HEAL, R.F.A.
Private REGINALD BIRD, 1/4 Duke of Cornwall Light Infantry.
Private CLAUDE SANDERCOCK, L. Battn.
Private THOMAS PEARSE WARD, 1/5 Somerset Light Infantry.
Private WILLIAM KNIGHT, Royal Army Veterinary Corps.
Private FREDERICK WERRING, 9th Worcestershire Regiment.
Private BARTON HEAL, 3rd Devonshire Regiment.
Private WILLIAM BRYANT JEWELL, Oxford and Bucks Light Infantry.
Trooper THOMAS FRANCIS GLADSTONE SANDERCOCK, Royal Scots Greys.
CHARLES COTTELL, Seaman, R.N.
Private STANLEY COWLING, Royal Berks.
Private OWEN FRY, R.F.A.
Private HERBERT SANDERCOCK, D.C.L.I.
Driver STEPHEN JOSE, Royal Engineers.
Driver DAVID MARTIN, Royal Engineers.
Driver CHARLES KNIGHT, R.F.A.
Private JOHN MARTIN, Machine Gun Corps.
Private WILLIAM AMBROSE SANDERCOCK, Royal North Devon Hussars.
Private SYDNEY MARTIN, Devonshire Regiment.
Private DONALD SANDERCOCK, R.A.F.
Private WILLIAM JOSE, 3rd Devon Regiment.
Private WILLIAM FRANCIS COOMBE, 3rd Devonshire Regiment.
Private RICHARD SANDERCOCK, Somerset Light Infantry.
Shoeing Smith ERNEST LYLE GLIDDON, 19th Hussars.
Pioneer WILLIAM RUSH, 7th Labour Battn., R.E.
FRANK ROGERS, S.S. Seaman Gunner, R.N.
Private THOMAS SANDERCOCK, R.E.
Private HARRY SANDERCOCK, Wilts Regiment.
JOHN BELLAMY, Seaman, R.N.

PRESENTED APRIL, 1920.

Driver Charles Knight
Royal Field Artillery

Driver Stephen Jose
Royal Engineers

Ernie Gliddon
Shoeing Smith, 19th Hussars

Reg Bird
Duke of Cornwall's Regiment

Richard Sandercock
Somerset L. I.

Bryant Jewell
Ox & Bucks L. I.

Mark Wickett
2nd Royal Irish Regiment

Ewart Gliddon
Royal Navy

John Bellamy
Royal Navy, Malta.

Edward Cory of Trelay
Royal Artillery.

Harry Polatch
Stoker, Royal Navy.

Tom Sandercock
Royal Engineers.

Ambrose Sandercock with friends
Royal North Devon Hussars.

St Gennys Volunteers leaving for the 1st World War.

Some of the Sandercock family at Roundhayes Farm. The gentleman in the uniform at the back is Mr Albert Sellers, who, having been wounded, was sent to Roundhayes as a "substitute".

Children at Congdon's Bridge

A souvenir mug
celebrating the
Coronation of King
George Vth and Queen
Mary.

The boys' class at St Gennys School.

The girls' sewing class with Miss Curnow.

A pony ride at the Haven.

Clarence Sandercock.

St Gennys Band - Christmas Postcard 1913.

Ewart Gliddon, Stan & Charles Cowling.

Brockhill Sunday School outing in 1912, with the two Sunday School teachers,
Mr Marchant and Mr Miller.

Class I & II at St Gennys School in 1913.

St Gennys Girls' Friendly Society Tableau, Ascensiontide, 1919.

Mrs Dorothy Teague
with William Sandercock
always known as 'Boxer'.

Ella Goodman

The Red Lion Inn, Tresparrett Posts.
In 1911 the owner, Mr Marshall, purchased at auction 12 acres, 1 rod and 19 perch for £420!

'Trevigue'

The Cycle Shop at 'Greenbank', Rosecare.

'Pentreath' with its beautifully laid out vegetable garden.

St. Catherine's, Tremoutha

Removing sand from the beach.

Red Devon cattle passing the Old Cottages.

The old bridge.

The Rev. A.G.D. Capel.
Vicar of St Gennys from 1918.

Mr Calvert.
Photographer and music teacher,
who took many of the postcards in
circulation today.

50616. St. Gennys Church, Cornwall.

St Gennys Church with the tower as it is today, restored by Edmund Sedding.

Harvesting at 'Roundhayes'.

BOUNDARY BEATING S. GENNYS 1913.

Beating the Bounds of St Gennys in 1913, it seemed the entire parish took part. The spelling of St Gennys on the boundary stone, below, is interesting.

BOUNDARY BEATING S. GENNYS 1913.

BOUNDARY BEATING S. GENNYS 1913.

BOUNDARY BEATING S. GENNYS 1913.

A child being bumped on the boundary stone at Tresparrett Posts. The idea was, that the children of the Parish should be 'bumped' so that they always knew where the boundary of their Parish was. Assisting with the 'bumping', Mr John Parnall, and in the background, a couple of lads waiting for the doubtful pleasure of a 'bump'.

Higher Dizzard, St Gennys.

Churchtown, St Gennys.

Lois Goodman with the Knight children, Frank, Ernie and Christine in 1912.

Granny Sandercock with 'Boxer', Ralph and Curls in 1916.

Brockhill Chapel in 1913. Mr Enoch Heal, Mr Rickard of Roundhayes, Mr H. Moyse of Pencuke and Mr W. Jenkins.

Threshing at the Coombe Barton.

'Cap'n'
William Edwards,
Auntie Bessie's
husband
and
his brother
Fred.

The Knight children at
Churchtown

Mr Tom Teague, husband of Mrs Dorothy Teague of 'Polmelyn'.

'Sandy Dick' carting sand.

The 'Donkey' and friends, the day before World War I broke out.

William Tilley,
father of
Alfred,
Lottie,
Monica
and
Roy.

John Parnall,
father of Roger Parnall.

'Belle Vue', Ludon

Mr Pinkney's ' Ça Va' on the beach in full sail!

The re-opening of Brockhill Chapel in 1913 by John Ward's aunt, Mrs Stephens, after the pews had been turned round to face east.

Maurice 'Nutty' Passmore

Dr Passmore and Mr Jewell in the garden at 'The Coombe Barton'

1921 - 1930

The very first beach shop

The 'Jewell's' out for a spin

Mr. J. J. Bell
sitting at his
desk in St. Gennys
Council School
in 1925.

Mr. A. A. Moore, one of the first AA patrolmen in the area.

Mr & Mrs Folley (Beatrice and Richard) with a very young Eric Folley

'Oaklands', Lovers' Lane.
One of the chalets through the Coombes,
originally owned by Richard Folley.

The postman at 'Trethew'. He would blow his whistle going down the valley, for the residents to meet him.

'Gunnedah' in the Boyle days, when it was known as 'Caravansera'

CHAPEL OF REMEMBRANCE, ST. JENNY'S CHURCH.

The Chapel of
Remembrance,
St Gennys Church
dedicated on Thursday,
May 19th 1921.

Cutting the tennis court
with 'Nellie'.
She wore special covers on
her hooves to prevent
damage to the court.

Visitors arriving
 at Sweets
for the
Summer
Holidays

Tremayna Chapel Sunday School Outing

Brockhill Chapel Sunday School Outing

The wedding of Rose Sandercock and Harry Polatch

.... and some of the guests and family relaxing in the fields at Hentervene

Approaching the Haven

CRACKINGTON HAVEN.

Coombe Barton,
Crackington Haven,
St. Gennys, Bude, R.S.O., Cornwall.

Telegrams :
Jewell, Haven, St.Gennys

Station :
OTTERHAM,
L.S.W.R.

Advertising The Coombe

Back: Gladys & Olive Medland, Ashley Rogers, Miss Wellington, Stanley Wickett, Emily Luxton and May Gliddon
Front: Caroline Skitch, William Rogers, Christine Knight and Wilfred Sandercock
St Gennys Council School's visit to The Empire Exhibition at Wembley in 1924. First prize for the best essay was awarded to Christine Knight.

St Gennys Band in 1925

.......and some of the early tourists who came to hear them

Harvesting
at
'Trencreek'...

..feeding
the chickens
in the yard...

......and ready
for
market

Mr Stone off to work

Nan Carss
with
Peter Mason

Mr & Mrs
Abe Hallett
who built
'Dorridge'

Dick
Goodman

The newly-built

'Benjys Field'

...and a young
Nan Robinson,
the owner for
many years

Ready for a swim!

Strangles Beach, Easter Sunday 1925

Churchtown Farm

Formal gardens at the Vicarage

Gunnedah under
construction
and some of those
who built it

The Infant Class at St Gennys Council School in 1926

Top row: Alfred Medland, Gordon Sandercock, John Medland, Thomas Hicks, Freddy Martin, Alfred Tilley, Claude Mason, Miss Gladys Medland (Teacher)
Middle row: Edward Cowling, Maude Furse (Martin), Joyce Ward (Gliddon), Irene Sandercock, Millie Alee
Bottom row: Margaret Ward (Punton), Edith Alee, Edna Sandercock (Inch), Mary Luxton (Hodge), Dorothy Rogers, Barbara Rogers (Jenkins)

67

Two more classes of St Gennys Council School during the nineteen twenties

Lawyer Stevens.
He lived at
'Rosecare Villa Farm'
and was a well known
and colourful
character.

Miss Luscombe and 'Spot'

The ancient oak tree at 'Treworgie'.
A popular playground for the school children of St Gennys.

The tinker,
Mr Kneebone,
outside
'Boskenna'

1931 - 1940

The wedding of Dorothy and Jack Northcott,
outside East Dizzard Farmhouse in 1937.

The recently built 'Gentle Knight', known then as 'Ashley House'.

The late Henry Hall, 3rd from the right, famous leader of the BBC Dance Band,
with friends in the hayfield at Churchtown.

Trial Hill
in the
1930's.

The Haven through the valley.

'St. Catherine's' and 'Tremoutha Cottage'.

Edna Sandercock, nanny to Buffy Gordon, married James Inch. Her father was the postman at Rosecare.

A very young Roger Anthony.

Harvesting at Churchtown.

St. Gennys School - 1935.

Higher Crackington with Trethew and Crackington Vean in the foreground.

Northern Door at Strangles Beach.

'Harvenna' as a Guest House in the 1930's.

David Pinkney diving from Gulley, 1933.

The South Tetcott Hunt meet at 'Nancemellan'.

Crackington Tennis Club in 1932.

Reg Wickett
and
Alf Tilley.

The Cowling family at
'Coxford'.

An aerial view of the Haven taken by Alan Parnall in 1939.
Notice the laid out vegetable fields on the side of Penkenna.

The Rev. Outram, far right, Vicar of St. Gennys from 1937 with Henry, Betty,
Majorie and Michael Hall, Mabel Gliddon, Mrs Colwill, Ned Colwill, Granny
Harker, Miss Syril, Mrs White and the dogs Bob and Patsy.

Miss Wellington who taught at
St. Gennys School.

Ruth Gliddon at the Manor.

William 'Uncle Bill' Marshall -
Peggy Chidley's father.

This window was commissioned in the 1930's, but never installed.

Rough sketch of Window to be placed in
— St Gennys Parish Church —
— as a War Memorial. —

Elizabeth, Kathleen, Ashley and Frank Rogers at 'Penwyth'.

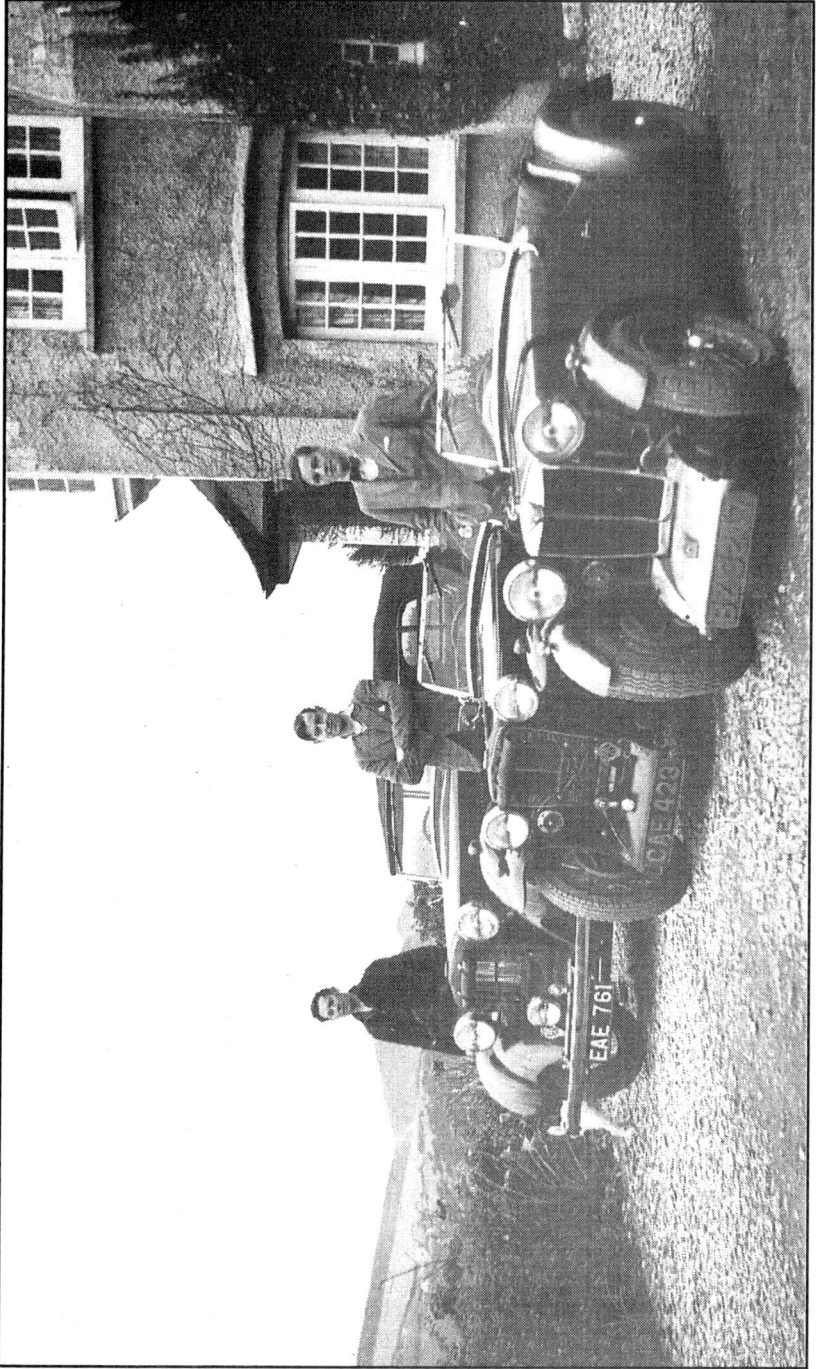

Alan and Dennis Parnall with Denis Lennon and their MG's outside 'Nancemellan'.

Inside St. Gennys Church in the gaslight days.

Another view of the Haven.

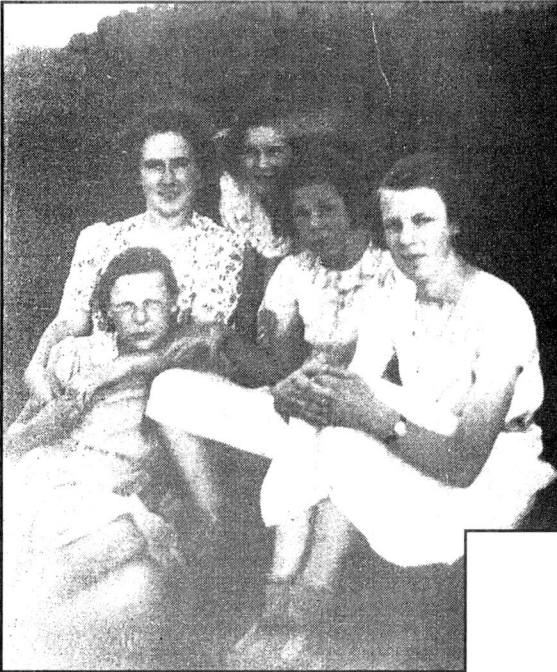

Margaret,
Edith,
Winifred
and
Muriel Ward
with
Monica Tilley.

Anne Dingley (now Barks) and her cousin
Jennifer Field on the beach in 1939.

A young
Maurice Teague
on the gate
at
'Gentle Knight'.

Leonard Ward's parents, Stephen and Edith, at 'Trethew'.

Haymaking in the Coombe Barton car park.

1941 - 1950

The first Carnival in 1945. Mr Bill Jenkins leads the procession and Mr John Biscombe and Mr William Hockin were footmen with the two greys, Tiny and Ruby.

The first Carnival Queen was Molly Gliddon
with Basil and Doug Sandercock postillions.

The Band leads some of the walkers at the first carnival .....

......and Alec Bright pushing son

One of the floats at the first Carnival. Stan Botterall was Henry VIIIth, with his wives, Dorothy Rogers, Ruby Coombe, Ena Burden, Bertha Gliddon, Eileen Tilley, and Betty Martin.

Above: Mrs Botterall, Mrs Dobson, Pam Chapman and Phyllis Partridge.

Left: Sylvia Mason, Mrs Ambrose Sandercock, Ruth and Alice Gliddon. First Carnival.

The 1948 Carnival Queen, Winifred Ward being crowned by Mrs Margaret Dingley, with her attendants - Iris Sandercock, Celia Ward, Rosemary Pickard and Ann Rogers.

Carnival Marshals Mr Barton Heal and Mr Bill Jenkins.

Float from a 1940's Carnival .....

... and Red Cross Detachment 168, with M. Rogers, E. Knight and D. Henderson.

The 1949 Carnival Queen, Hilda Cowling with her attendants Cecily Biscombe, Celia Ward, Iris Sandercock and Margaret Mason.........

.... and the 1949 Carnival Marshall, Mr Heal riding Julie.

May 1944. Crackington Platoon of the Home Guard under Lieut. R.J. Burden won the shield for the best trained platoon in the Coastal Battalion.

Edward Cowling, Stan Wickett, Jack Gliddon, Charlie Gliddon, Arthur Hay, Mark Luxton, Harry Sandercock, Wilfred Jose, Doug Bennett, Bill Lee. Brian Ward, Gordon Heal, Will Goldsworthy, Barton Heal, Stanley Bird, Arthur Burden, Cecil Piper, Richard Teague, Dan Boundy, Will Bellamy. Joe Tape, Stan Sandercock, Charles Chapman, Harold Brown, Sprig Barkwell, Bert Gliddon, John Cowling, Jack Northcott, Ken Sutton, Tom Matthews, Clarence Sandercock, Alec Bright, Reg Burden, Roy Dymond, Jack Teague, John Ward, Harry Chapman.   from above Ted Rogers, Leslie Bird.

93

Plaque of Remembrance in St Gennys Church for those who did not return from World War II.

Part of The Victory Parade.

Leonard Ward,
Radar Operator
R.A.F.

'Boxer' Sandercock,
Royal Engineers.

Richard Teague,
Duke of Cornwall's Light Infantry.

Alan and Denis
Parnall,
R.A.F.

William Goldsworthy,
'Catchgate', St Gennys,
with awards and merits
won by him.
In the centre is a certificate
from the King and Queen for
wartime service as a nursing
orderly. Very few in the
country won this award.

Ruth and Bert Gliddon, the only serviceman's wedding to be held in St Gennys Church during the second World War. Officiated by the Rev. Outram.

Les and Stan Bird in the Home Guard.

Alf Tilley serving in the R.A.S.C. before returning from France and transferring to the R.E.M.E.

Bert Gliddon serving in Gibraltar.

German E Boat, built in Bremen in 1942 and wrecked at Crackington Haven in 1946. Its engine room telegraph can be seen in The Coombe Barton Inn.

MV Escaut - Dutch ship bombed and strafed by German aircraft and beached by Capt. Nicol Kuizenga at Cancleave Strand. A serious fire in her cargo burned for four days.

The captain and some of the crew of the Escaut with Lottie Tilley, to whom they presented a tea set in appreciation of her care of them.

W.R.V.S. Soup Kitchen.

Evacuees from Clapham,
South London.............

.... in the
vicarage garden.......

.......and in the
valley collecting
clay for pottery.

Wartime defences on the beach at Crackington with Monica Griffs, Michael O'Riley, Mollie Gliddon (nee Harper) and Wilfred Jose.

The lads
boxing behind
the Institute.

Norman Pickard,
Stan Bird,
Tony Sandercock,
Fred Bird

Mr Frank Ward
at Flanders
with Violet
and her foal.

St Gennys Band in 1949 when they won the Cup at Stenalees.

St Gennys School in 1948...................

........................and in 1949

St Gennys Church 1946 from a Christmas card sent by the Rev. Outram.

Back: Philip Tape, Edgar Heal, Tony Sandercock, Douglas Trewin.
Front: Lloyd Sandercock, Arthur Smeeth, Alan Hancock, Walter Polatch.

Pam and John Ward's wedding day. The yard gate at East Dizzard Farm was blocked by 'friends!'

The Bird boys with Mum at 'Oakleigh', Pencuke.

A Crowle's coach - note the telephone number!

Great Grandma and Granfer Sandercock's Diamond Wedding in 1943.

The Billiard Room at Crackington Manor.

Alan Zoeftig

Paul Tilley

Lloyd Cowling
and
Doug Trewin.

British Legion parading past Crackington Vean led by St.Gennys Band.

The river
at
Crackington
Haven.

Lover's Walk.

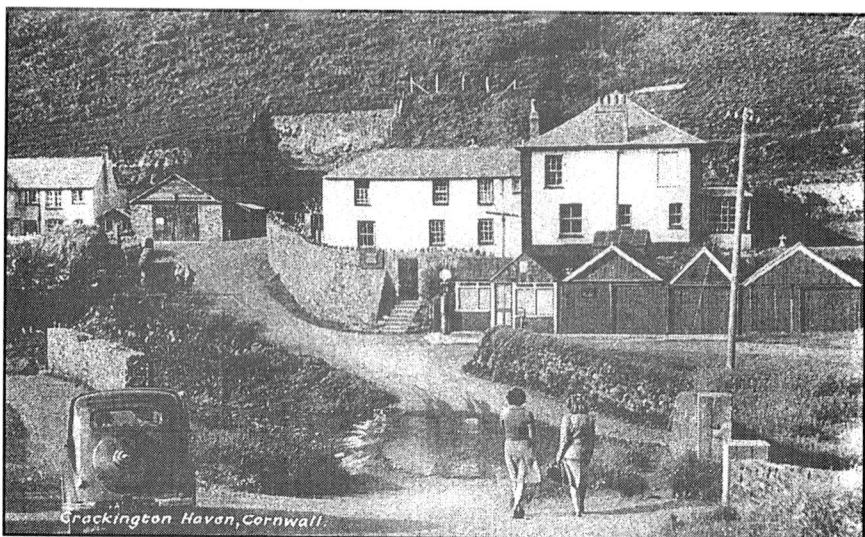

The water-splash at Crackington Haven.

Reginald 'Curls' Sandercock with Ambrose, Gladys and baby Carol.

1951 - 1960

The laying of the foundation stone for the Crackington Institute by Mr Roger Parnall, on a site given by Mr Frank Ward...........................

........and the completed building.......

..........replacing the railway carriage in the background

The new Crackington Institute opened by Judge Scobell-Armstrong, CBE and

..........honouring Julia Tilley, with Victorian charm, who presented him with a memento of the occasion, and an equally gracious curtsey.

The handing over of the key by Mr Thomas Teague and ....

.... the ladies who prepared the celebratory meal. Evelyn Ward, Ruth Biscombe, Janey Botterall, Gladys Medland, Barbara Rogers, Dorothy Rogers, Vera Stuttaford, Mary Teague, Pam Ward, Millie Chapman and Mary Ward.

Rex Ward
presenting
a
bouquet
to Mrs West Stephens
of Rugby,
who opened
the sale of work
and stalls.

The Mayor of Launceston addressing the guests.

Parishioners enjoying the occasion.

Listening to the vote of thanks by Mr W.T. Tilley, the Institute President.

1st Cornwall Lone Guides
formed by Mrs Bloomer.
There were two patrols,
Puffins and Choughs.
Ann Rogers,
Shirley Northcott,
Ann Sandercock,
Jocelyn Tape,
Margaret Mason.

Long-a-row field from St Mary's before it became Long-a-Row Close.

Charlie Cowling with Flower and Blossom.

Sheep dipping.

Cecil Piper ploughing with the Cory's horses, and........................

.... Jim Cory tractor ploughing.

Roundhayes transformed into a pub for the ploughing match, and Jack Gliddon receiving his trophy.

Frank Ward and son John behind the wagon, with Alan Hancock and Father Johnny making the rick, on Barton.

Three generations
of
Heards.
Mr John, Mr Jack
and Richard.

Confirmation at St
Gennys with Bishop
Wellington. The group
includes Bert & Ruth
Gliddon and Jim Cory.

A very
young Rex
Ward.

Snow on Cambeak, February 1956.

Mrs Bunney with Peter, Tom and friends on Haven Bridge.

Ena
and
Richard
Brown

Wedding days in the fifties

Jean
and
Gordon
Teague.

Construction of the new bridge in 1954.

The temporary footbridge and the newly opened, completed bridge - 1954.

Cap'n Edwards and his trusty grey Ferguson tractor.

Off to work.

Bill Dymond, Jack Gliddon, Char Cowling, Barton Heal, Jim Cory, Sam Smith, Cecil Piper, Len Wonnacott, Ashley Rogers & Stewart Dymond threshing at Penwyth.

John and Simon Rogers

A young Roy Tilley

Norman Pickard in The Somerset Light
Infantry, serving in Malaya.

Roger Anthony, Royal Marines,
aboard H.M.S. Triumph.

The school garden.

Church Fete in the Vicarage walled garden.

St Gennys School Canteen with Mrs Pearce - a wonderful cook.

'A Midsummer Night's Dream' at St Gennys School.

St Gennys School - 1952

St Gennys School - 1958

Claude Mason
with his
young
apprentice.

The Band playing
Christmas Carols
around the parish.

St Gennys Silver Band wearing their new uniforms, with Carnival Queen Jocelyn Tape, attendants Sheila Piper and Ann Rogers, and the Ladies' Committee.

Edith Ward crowning Carnival Queen, Eileen Clarke with her attendants Shirley Howell and Betty Newham and child attendants Brenda Biscombe and Diana Heard.

Great Granny Sandercock and Granny Ambrose
enjoying an ice-cream at the Carnival.

Mr Herbert Jenkins opening a Fifties carnival, and ....

........................a Snow White float.

Trevor, Peter and Christopher Biscombe, St Gennys Carnival, August 1951.

1953 Carnival Queen Nancy Crowle with attendants Jean Cowling, Ena Burden, Pamela Gliddon and Dennis Tape.

The new organ at Brockhill Methodist Church. Mr W. Parnall visiting organist from Stratton with the Rev. Alner, Mr Tom Ward, Harry Teague, Richard Teague, Mr F. Ward, Dorothy Rogers, Gladys Medland, Ruth Biscombe & Margery Rogers.

The re-opening of Tremayna Methodist Church in 1953.

The ladies of the church at Tremayna's re-opening.

The Rev. Stainer Smith with John Henry Gliddon and friends at the re-opening of
Tremayna Methodist Church.

Rosecare Green in the Nineteen Fifties.

St Gennys Band entertaining in the Haven.

Cattle crossing the new bridge

Flanders Farm in the 1950's

The Royal British Legion Hall decorated for the Coronation celebrations in 1953.

Brian Teague, the first apprentice electrician in St Gennys.

Electric power first came to St Gennys in 1956.

1961 - 1970

The re-opening of the British Legion Hall by the County Chairman, Mrs Asher, in September 1965.

Mrs Asher being presented with a bouquet.

Mrs Phyllis Cory
British Legion
Poppy Organiser
for 57 years.

Two very young poppy sellers.

Outside Tremayna Methodist Church at the Centenary Celebrations.

Tremayna Methodist Church decorated for the Centenary Celebrations in 1962.

Rev. John K. Lockyer,
Minister at the time.

The 100 year old Tremayna in 1962.

St Gennys Silver Band playing at a Band Fete in the garden of 'Grey Roofs'.

St Gennys Playgroup in the 60's. It was started by Rosemary Freestone, Pat Anthony, Pat Preller and Milly Brown.

Enjoying a Christmas drink in the Coombe Barton. Peter Treleaven, Brian Breyley, Roy Breyley, Henry Biscombe, Bill Reynolds, Rosemary Freestone and Cyril Lyons, with Phil Freestone at the rear.

St Gennys School in 1962, taken at the school's Open Day during National Education Week.

The retirement of Mr and Mrs Bloomer in 1967. They had been at St Gennys
School for twenty six years

Mrs Lane's class at St Gennys School.
Richard Ash, Kevin Waters, Michael Northcott, Charles Tippett, Lawrence
Loader, John Freestone, Jeremy Teague, Ian Freestone, David Sandercock,
Alison Tape, Hilary Chidley, Angela Biscombe, Lynne Teague, Rachel Anthony,
Teresa Northcott, Ruth Anthony, Harriet Preller.

St Gennys School ready for an outing in 1965.

Churchtown, with the school canteen in the foreground.

The Rev. Parish with a visiting clergyman at St Gennys Church.

The first surf board seen in Crackington Haven. Leonard Ward in action in the early 1960's.

Carnival Queen Joy Rigby-Jones with her attendants Zelah Gliddon and Jill Crabb, accompanied by Richard Rigby-Jones.

THE "MAD HATTERS" TEA PARTY

The Mad Hatter's Tea Party at the 1969 Carnival.
John, Willy and Ian Freestone with Susan Trewin.

Carnival Queen Carolyn Biscombe with attendants
Angela Biscombe and Alison Tape in 1969.

'Those Were The Days'. 1966 Carnival.

Lynne Teague presenting a bouquet to Joy Rigby-Jones who had crowned
Carnival Queen Marion Bennett. .

Bonnie & Clyde at a 60's Carnival.

Tony Sandercock and Adrian Ward
beating the postal strike!

George Cowling with the Freestone boys at crib time.

Re-roofing 'Top Cottage' at 'Hallagather', in 1963. Now know as 'Hannah's Cottage', where Mrs Esme Hannah once lived.

Tom Pearce's old grey mare carting Ronald Sandercock, Peter Biscombe, Roger Teague, Trevor Biscombe, John Rogers, Stan Smith and Tom Polatch to Widecombe Fair.

The 'Pirates of Crackington' driven by Bill Bragg.

Jonathan and Mark Parnall.

Roger Teague, Tony Sandercock, John Rogers,
Trevor Biscombe and 'Curls' Sandercock

The Haven in the sixties

The last combine used at 'Hallagather'.

St Gennys Church Fete in the vicarage grounds,
with Dr. and Mrs Gordon manning a stall.

The Biscombes

| Henry | Bill | Charles | John |
| Ruth | Norah | Audrey | Monica |

Campers in Dam Field.

Stuart Biscombe at
a ploughing match.

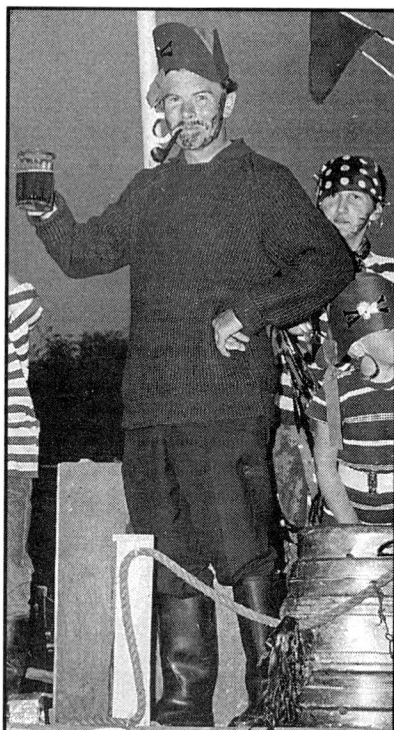
Mike Preller aboard
the pirate ship.

Rachel Anthony lambing.

Sheila Folley
on a carnival float.

1971 - 1980

An aerial view of Higher Crackington before Brockhill Estate was built, and...........

.....Jill Crabb sitting on the wall at 'Minith' with open fields across the valley.

Brockhill Estate with the workers' caravans standing on the site of No. 2, Haven Road and

under construction

over several years

in the early nineteen seventies.

Gathering for the start of the 1977 'Beating the Bounds' to commemorate the Queen's Silver Jubilee.

167

The marshalling area for the walkers.

Walking the 'bounds'

Frank Tape and Char Cowling 'bumping' Herbert Jenkins.

St. Gennys Church in the snow.

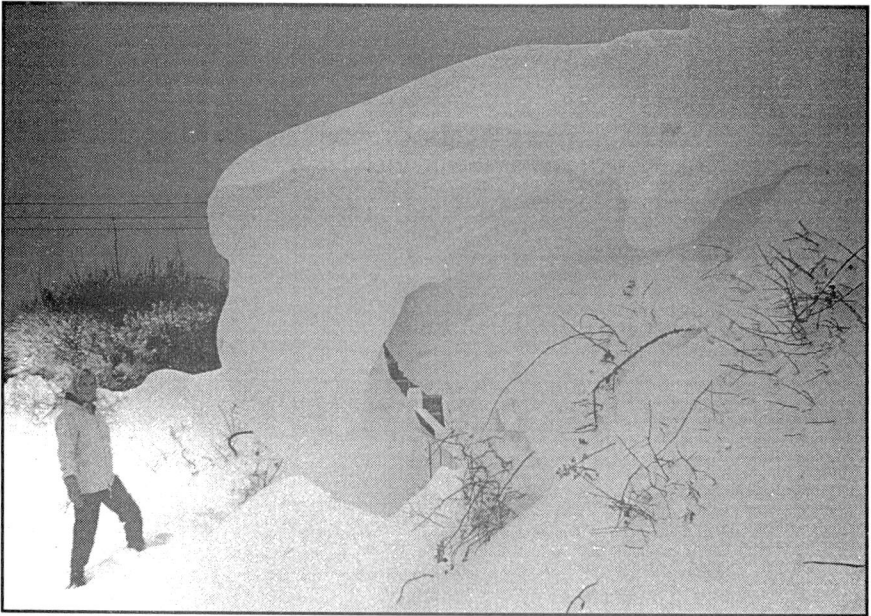

Mrs Dennler after the great blizzard of 1978 at the end of Flanders Lane. The Wards lost 32 sheep, buried on Penkenna.

The motor yacht 'Casketa'. She anchored off Crackington Haven in September 1973. The crew of two came ashore in a rubber dinghy, but during the night she parted her cable and drove ashore. She was refloated a week later and taken to Padstow.

170

The 1979 Carnival Queen, Nicola Bird with her attendants -
Louise Kendling, David Heard and Jon Spettigue.

Steptoe and Son at the 1978 Carnival.

Mr Mason leading the 1979 Carnival

A ninteen seventies Carnival Queen, Michelle Teague
with her attendants Cherry Smeeth and Tamsin Bunney.

St Gennys Silver Band in the late 70's with their conductor Mr Cyril Payne, B.Mus., F.T.C.L., L.T.C.L., and a former music producer of the BBC.

ST. GENNYS SILVER BAND

Memories

ST. GENNYS PARISH in CORNWALL

Cover of the record the Band made in 1979, recorded by Sentinel Records of Penzance. The album was sent all over the world and its sale financed new instruments.

Four
generations
of Sandercocks,
taken at
'Roundhayes'.

St Gennys School which closed in 1975.

Opening the 'Burden Trust' Car park in 1979.

Mrs Dorothy Moores, President of the Royal British Legion, Ladies Section, presenting the Poppy Badge to Mrs Bird, one of the founder members.

George Potier and his World Record Porbeagle Shark of 465 lbs. landed at Crackington Haven in June 1978.

Aftermath of the blizzard in 1978.

Kate Tilley with Monica, Alfred, Lottie, Eileen and Roy, taken in 1972.

Bringing mains water to Lansweden in 1975

Dick Gliddon and **Rusty**

Presentation of mugs, commemorating
25 years of the Institute.

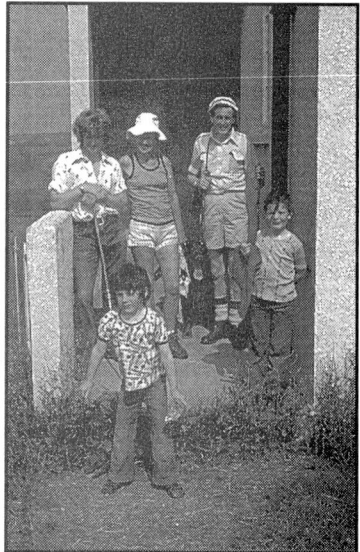
Ready for a Band walk.

The wedding
of Joyce and
Alan Heard
in September,
1971.

St Gennys W.I.
on a coastal
walk in 1980.

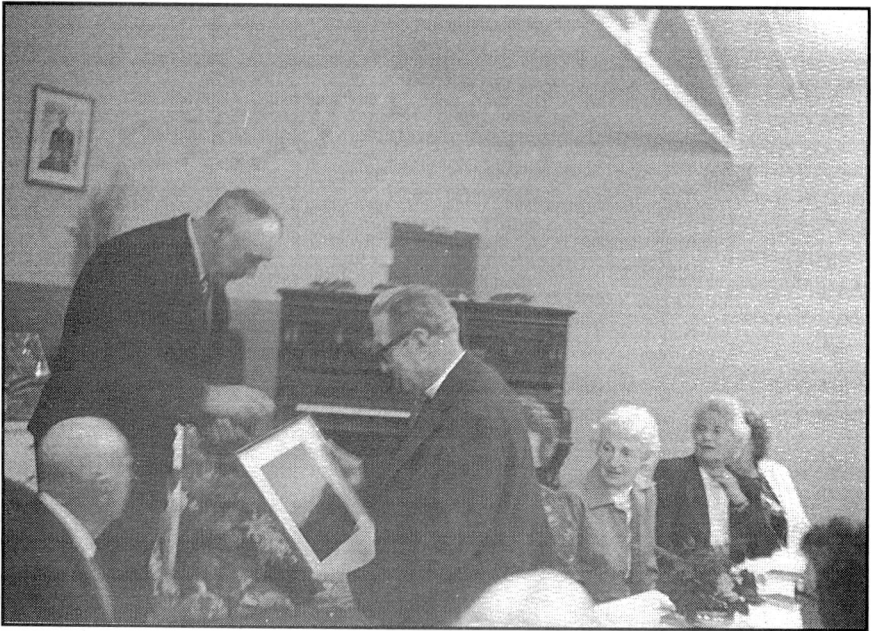

The retirement of the Rev. Lovell.

Victoria Berry, Cherry Smeeth and Michelle Teague
with their awards at a Red Cross presentation.

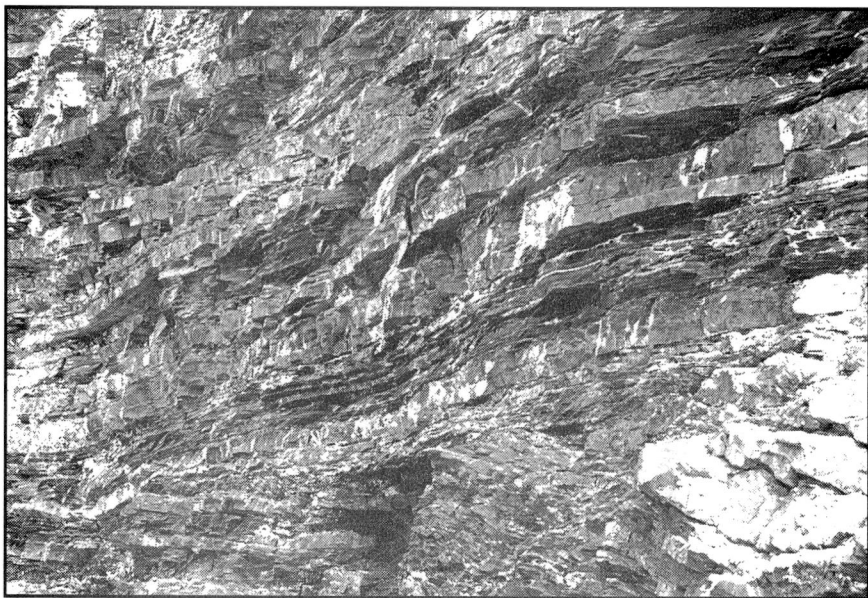

The Crackington Formation which continues to attract geological study groups.

Charlie Tippett and Lawrence Loader with the Warby boys.

A panoramic view of a 1970's Carnival in the Coombes.

The newly-opened Snooker Club and below,
the space that became the present bar.

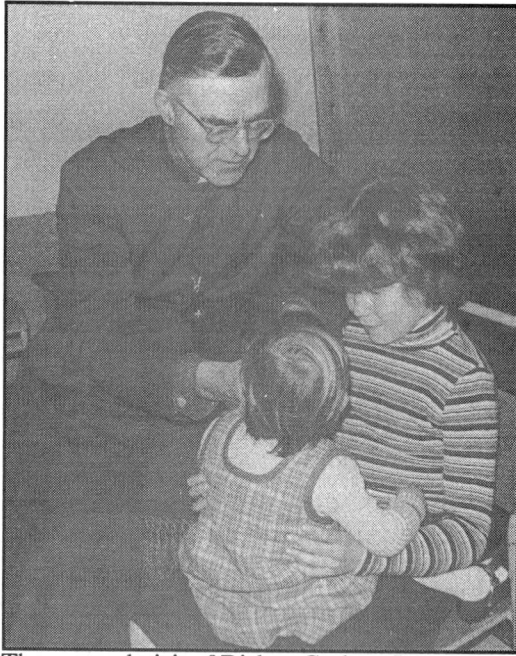

The pastoral visit of Bishop Graham Leonard......

..........with the Rev. Vere Lawrence, the churchwardens Tony Mount and John Towl, and Jeremy Dowling, the interregnum deacon.

1981 - 1990

The re-slating
of St Gennys
Church by
the Teagues,
in 1983.

Continuing the work.....

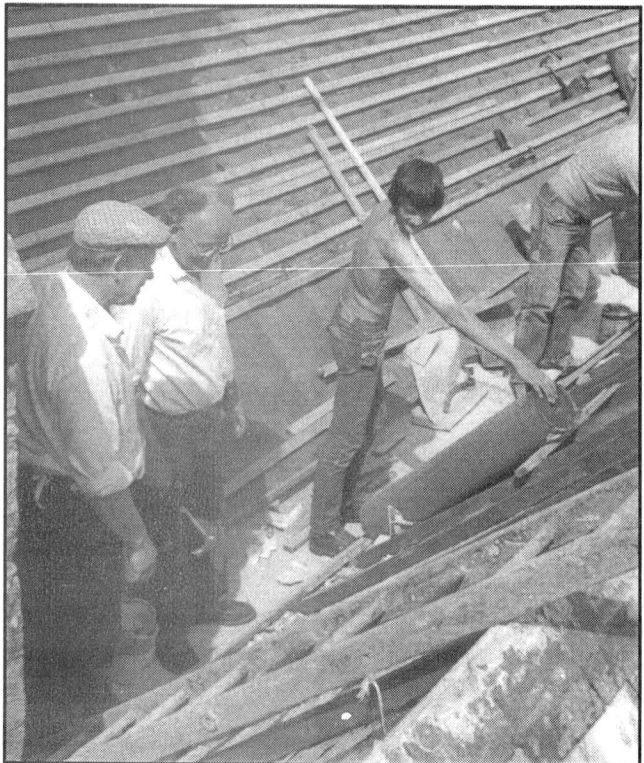

.... on the church roof .

Jeremy Dowling, interregnum lay preacher, signing the two thousand, seven hundred and seventy sixth slate during the roof re-slating.

St Gennys Playgroup taken in 1983 with Joan Beart.

St Gennys Youth Club with Maureen Taylor, taken on a trip to St Ives.

The building of Crackington Haven Surf Club.

St Gennys W.I. at their Silver Jubilee in 1981.

The First Cornwall Air Ambulance landing in the field behind the Institute.

Pat Sheer, Red Cross leader and ....

...... some of the Cadets she had under her wing.

Mary Rogers with Ann and John, being thanked by Drs. Weir and Young
for handing out prescriptions over many years.

Molly Teague, on behalf of The Busy Bees, with Drs. Weir and Garrod. The
Busy Bees raised money to buy the surgery couch.

St Gennys Silver Band and its Youth Section in 1987.

Some of the ladies who made kneelers for St Gennys Church, led by Mrs Hellen Knight, and ......

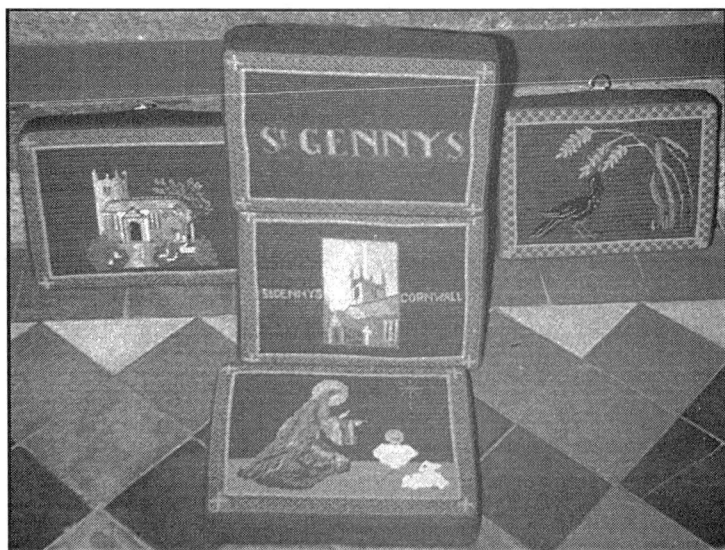

.... some of the kneelers they produced.

Mrs Moores
and
David
outside
the shop.

Nicola Cooper
presenting the 'Top of
the Parish' trophy to
'The Farmers': Dorothy
Munday, Oliver Tippett
and Rex Ward.

Kelly and Nelson in the snow.

Presentation of trophies at a Snooker Club dinner in the Coombe Barton. Neil Morrison, Peter Edgar, Howard Williamson, Barry Bird and David Teague with Jack Walton, Chairman.

Sausage Sizzle on the beach for ARC, the Arthritis and Rheumatism Council. Wing Commander Peter Farlow of Roundhayes started the fund raising for ARC assisted here by Jean Hayward, Marjorie Walton, Dorothy Moores, Connie Tilley and Carol Attwood.

St Gennys Quiz Team of Maggie Folley, Len Ward and Henry Boettinger, with Radio Cornwall's Duncan Warren, receiving their certificates after winning The Calor Gas Village Quiz Competition.

The Quiz Team, joined by Carol Cook, who representing Cornwall, beat Devon in the inter-county quiz.

St Gennys Ladies Choir conducted by Deryn Roberts.

Planting a tree in the Coombes on behalf of St Gennys Playgroup
during 'National Tree Planting Year' in 1984.

Some of the Carnival Queens and attendants of the eighties..

Emily and Rachel Herr.

Alison Turner and Brooke Tippett

Joanna Lees.

Carnival in the eighties. Eileen Johnson, Dorothy Scoffham, Vivien Cornish, Florrie Cambridge and Barbara Jenkins.

Paul Teague and Simon Rogers

Rob Sandercock as Bernie Clifton.

Reg Burden opening the 1983 Carnival.

The Falcon coach at Tresparrett Posts with Peggy and Horace Chidley.
The coach was driven by Mr Bill Tucker.

Mrs Mary Rogers ready for her trip to London where she was presented to the Queen and Prince Philip. For nearly 35 years she organised whist drives, jumble sales and held a collection box for The British Sailor's Society, and for this work, was recognised by the Royal family at a service in Fishmonger's Hall, London.

Street Party at Higher Crackington for the wedding of Prince Charles and Lady Diana Spencer.

Crackington Haven Short Mat Bowls Club in the Institute.

Tree planting in the Burden Trust Car Park by F. Mole, G. Northcott, B. Gliddon, V. Taylor, R. Anthony & T.Biscombe.

The demolition of St Gennys School canteen.

Bert Gliddon and Norah Jewell carrying the standards of St Gennys British
Legion and Ladies Section, at Windsor.

A Nativity service in St Gennys Church.

The retirement of Dr Young. Mrs Rogers and Mrs Chidley made the presentation accompanied by Mr John Ward, Chairman of the Parish Council.

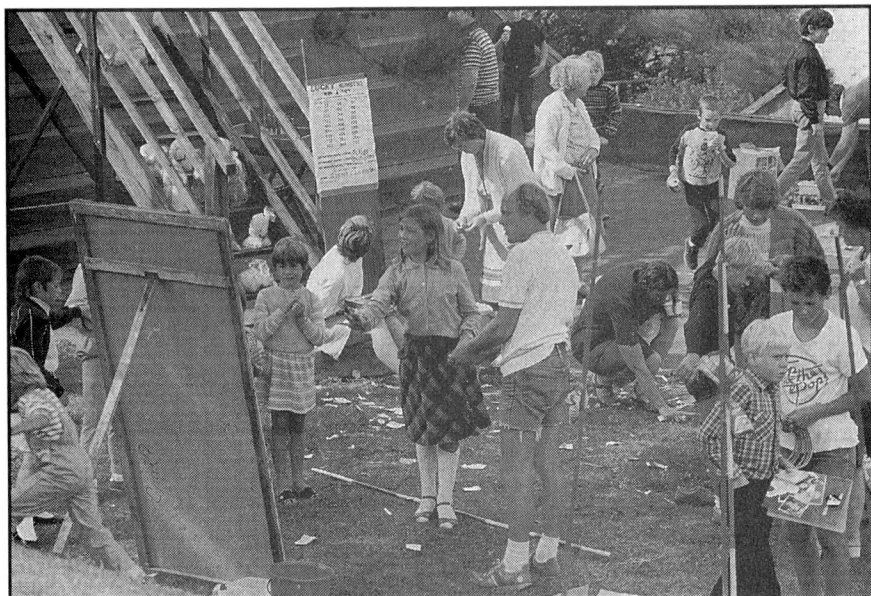
A Church Fete at Crackington Manor.

Charlie Tippett and Ian Freestone at Trial Hill. This hill is a regular feature of the annual Lands End Trial.

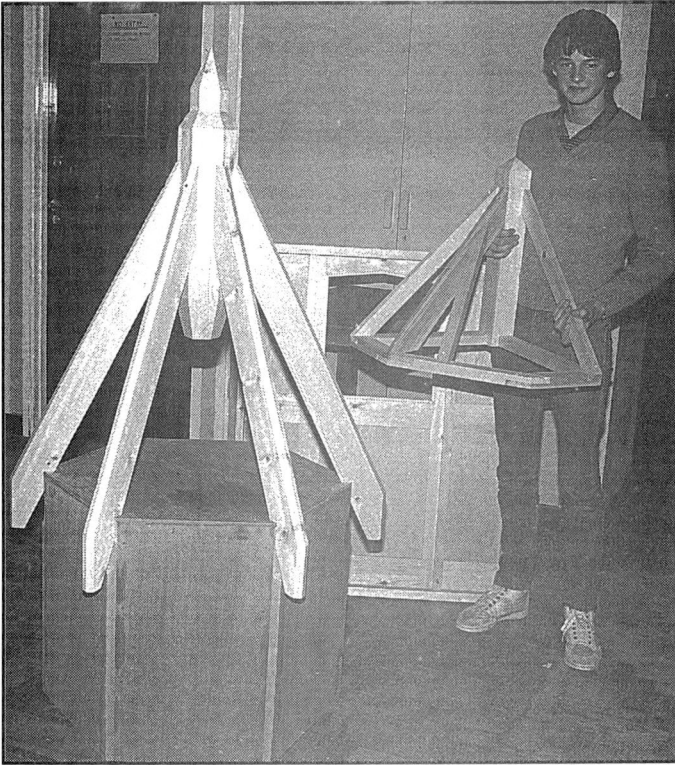

Paul Teague with the model he made for the City and Guilds examination...

... and the City and Guilds first prize medal he won
for the carpentry and joinery craft.

The four doctors who served St Gennys in the 80's, at Dr. Young's retirement.

The Bowling Club team at the last of the 'Top of the Parish' quizzes.

1991 - 2000

The Parish Council planting trees at St Gennys Church to celebrate the 50th anniversary of the end of WW II.

Leonard Ward was made a Cornish Bard in 1999 for his services to Community Life in Cornwall. He took the name 'Map Plu Gennys' (son of the Parish of St Gennys).

Ray Reardon, six times World Snooker Champion, with some of the Snooker Club's Juniors.....

....and with Roger Teague, Chairman of Crackington Snooker Club, at the opening of the new extension.

The new extension to the Institute which now houses two full-size snooker tables.

A charity bike-ride which raised £948-55 for Telethon '92.

The filming of 'Amy Foster' on Barton at the top of Penkenna.

Crackington Surf Life Saving Club Nippers.

Players in the 1999 Coombe Barton Invitation Golf Tournament, and ....

... the winner, Andy Etheridge, with host and hostess, John and Nicola Cooper.

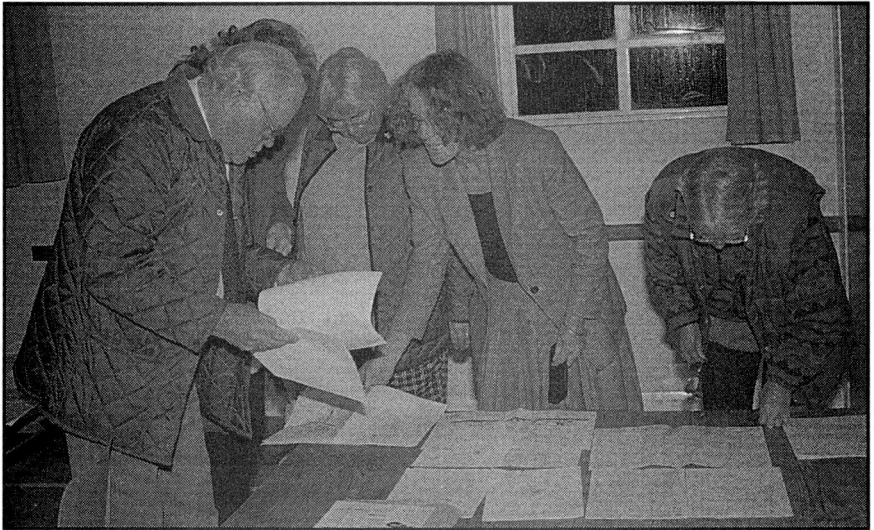

A Parish Council meeting in 1999.

Matthew Tilley, 1994 Craft Student of the Year,
and with his special award received in 1995 for
Construction Training Group Carpenter/Joiner.

Paul Anderson, who received The Emile Robin Award For Seamanship and an award from The Royal Humane Society, after the rescue of the crew from the Maged-H which sank off Greece. Only one soul was lost.

Henry Boettinger,
'Mastermind'
runner-up in 1995, with
question master,
Magnus Magnusson.

Geoff Seccombe,
Managing Editor of
'The Post' thanking
retiring correspondent
Mary Gliddon for her
reporting of the
happenings from St
Gennys over a quarter
of a century.

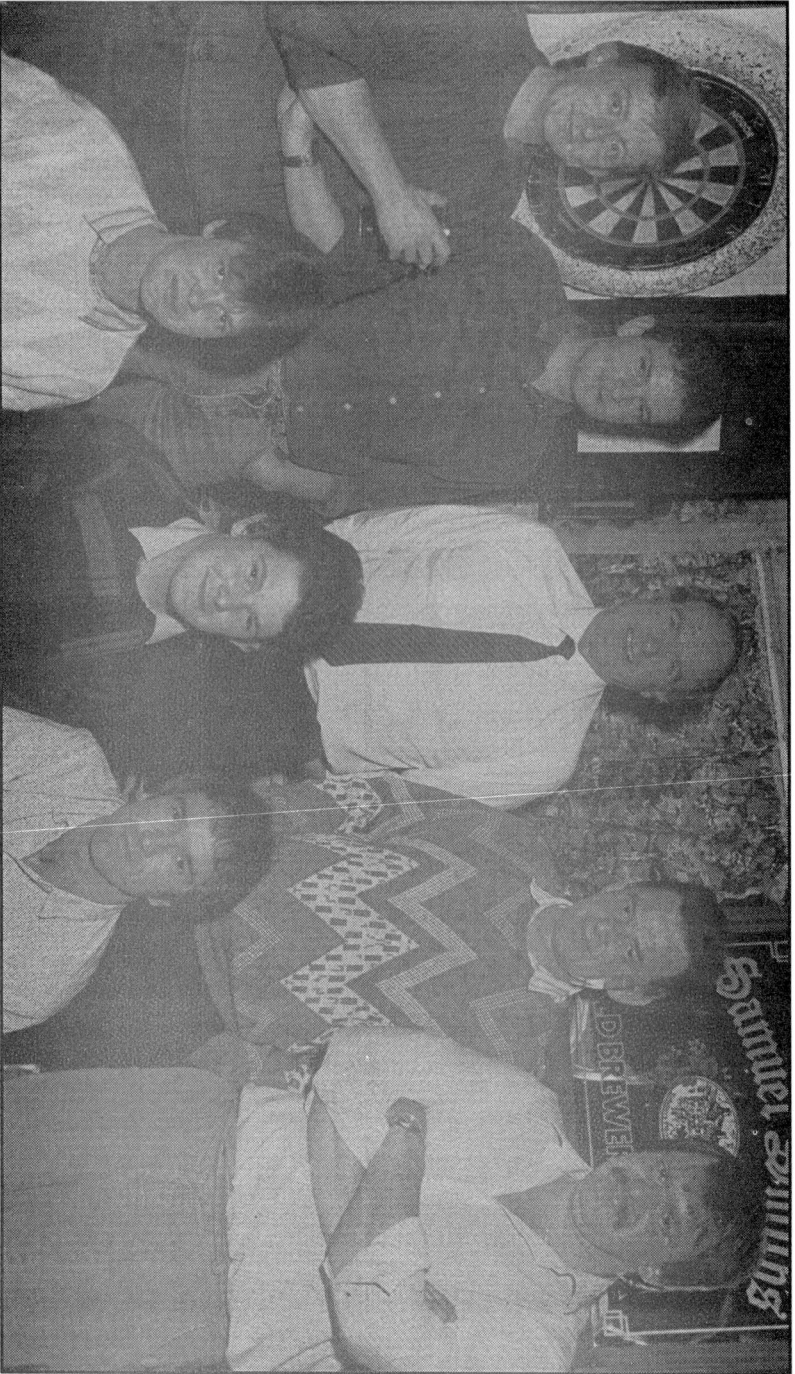

Coombe Barton Darts Team during a charity competition.

The sinking of the yacht Mary E off Penkenna Point in 1996. Her sole crew member was lifted off the rocks to safety, and after failing to refloat her she was stripped of all useful fittings and left to break up.

Nick Cooper with an 8lb. bass he caught off Penkenna.

John Scott with son Alan and daughter-in-law Kay.
The last wedding of the century at St Gennys Church.

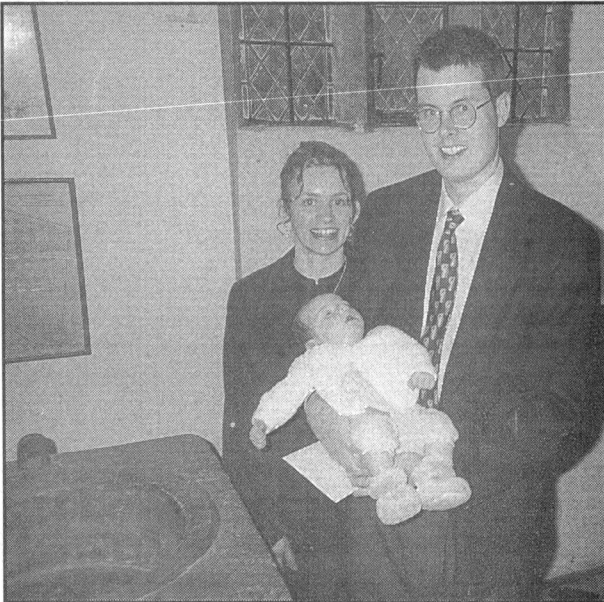

Alison and Richard Wilson with Nathaniel Isaac.
The last christening of the century at St Gennys Church.
Alison is the daughter of Ray and Shirley Dawe.

Confirmees with Bishop Graham.
The last confirmation of the century at St Gennys Church.

Flower festival for the 150th anniversary of Brockhill Chapel. This arrangement
'The Head That Once Was Crowned With Thorns' was created by Cheryl Ward.

Armistice Day 1999. The St Gennys Silver Band drummers leading the parade...

..... and the Rev. Roger Greene, Methodist Minister and Fr. Julian Davey, greeting the marchers at St Gennys Church.

Chairman of the Parish Council, Tony Herr, during the campaign to stop the illegal removal of stones and rocks from the beach.

James Comber and Paul Ferris were selected for the Cornwall Rugby Development Academy.

Coombe Barton Cricket Team, winners of The Flowers Tintagel Sunday Knockout Competition in the nineties.

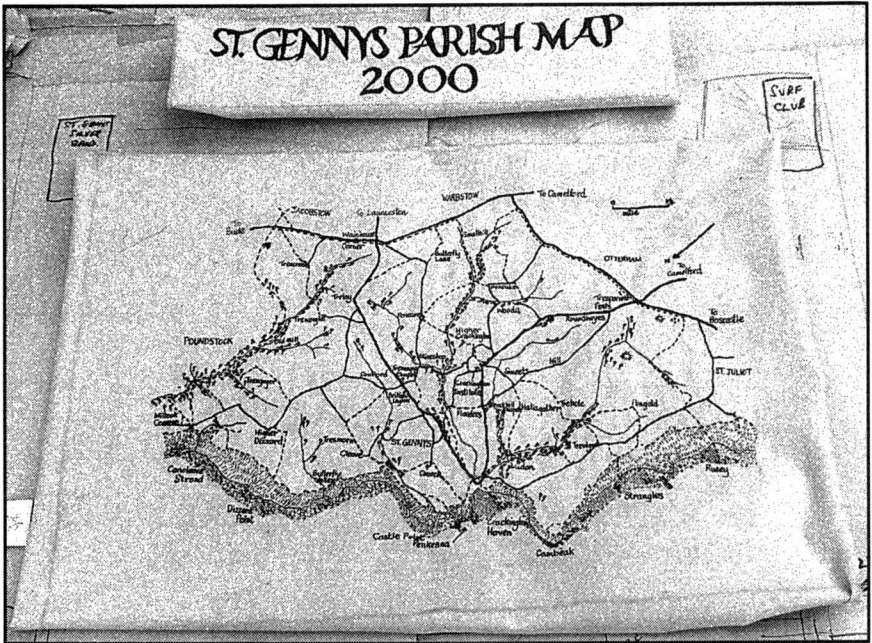

The beginning of the embroidered 'Parish Map' project for the Millennium - the idea of Jen Spettigue and Maggie Folley, and below, Angela Berry and Maggie discussing progress.

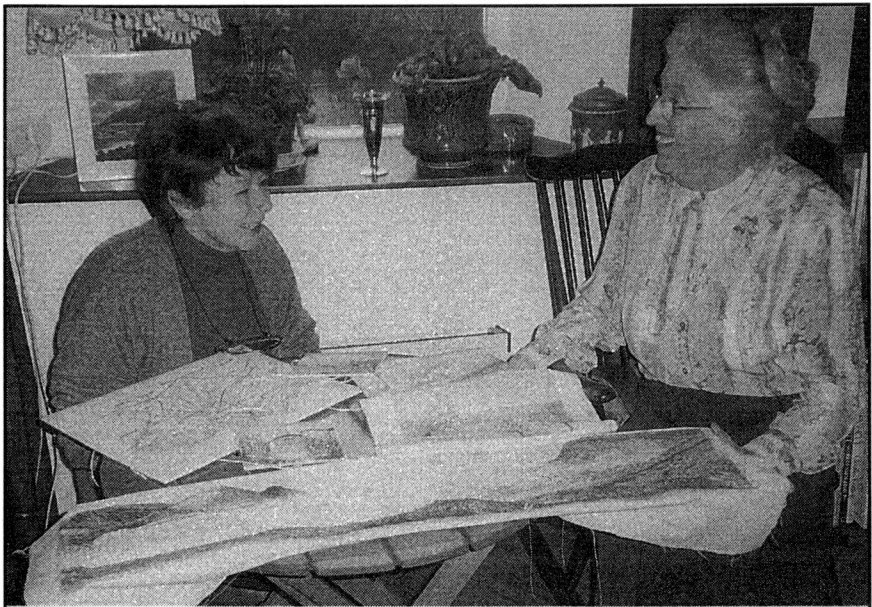

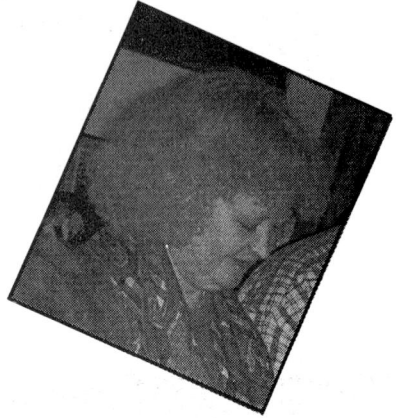

Some of the ladies

at work on

the parish map.

The finished Parish Map.

St Gennys Band playing in the Haven at a combined churches & chapels'
'Songs of Praise'.

Crackington Haven Tennis Club.

The Crackington Choristers with their conductor Buffy Wade in 1999.

The 60th Anniversary Lunch of the Ladies Section of St Gennys Royal British Legion.

Fr. Philip Randall, Vicar of St Gennys from 1987 to 1997.

Heidi Clelland and 'Magic', a successful equestrian combination.

Jacky Allan, a local carver and lettercutter who, for over fifteen years, has been making memorials, sundials and name plates on slate.

1990's Carnival Queens and attendants.

Abigail Stewart

Lisa and Emma Vanstone

Charlotte Bunney, with Lindsay Skinner and Keri Horwell

Anna Ward with Victoria Tippett and Lisa Vanstone.

St. Trinians!

Granny Queen and Granny in Waiting

Me and my gal

St Gennys Horticultural Show

The Horticultural Show Committee members.
Jeanette Turner, Mabel Gliddon and President, Reg Burden.

Diversity at Trevigue, combining conservation, farming and tourism.

Francis Crocker receiving English Nature's SSSI award, for Management of Cliffland, from Paul Tyler, MP......

.... and Gayle and Janet Crocker whose restaurant at Trevigue won the 1999 'Taste of the West' award.

John and Pam Ward ready to leave for Buckingham Palace as guests at The Royal Garden Party given by the Queen and Prince Philip to celebrate their Golden Wedding Anniversary. Couples married in 1947 were invited.

John and Marian Astley with Shirley Dawe in the village shop.

Jubilee Club Christmas lunch at ' Trencreek'.

The telescope made by Peter Westoby for the Eclipse, in his garden at Rosecare.

'Cream Teas' at 'Pendennis'.

The final nativity play of the century at St Gennys Church.

OUT with the OLD.......

.....IN
with the
NEW.

Millennium Party at the Snooker Club.

238

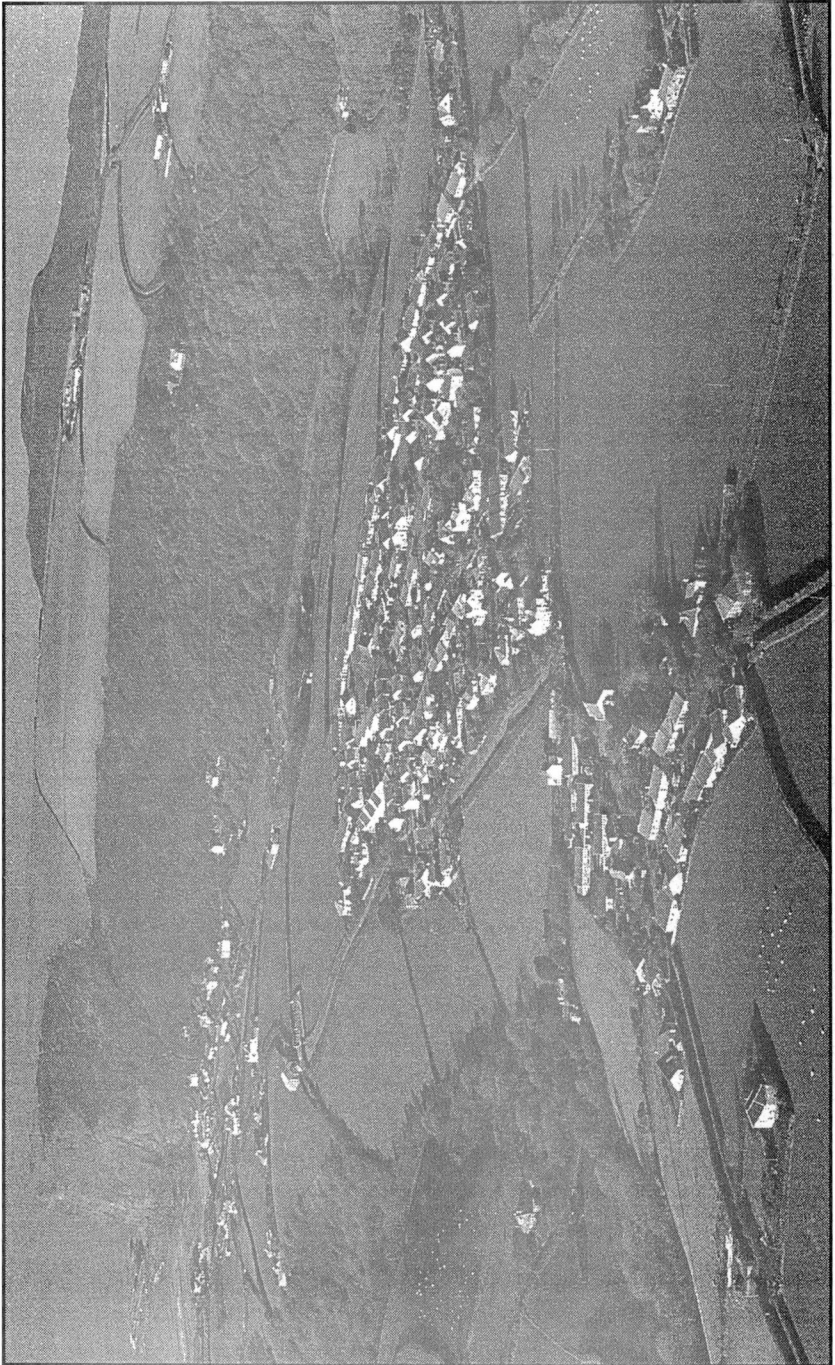

An aerial view of St Gennys and Crackington Haven taken in 1997.

The
Book
Team.....

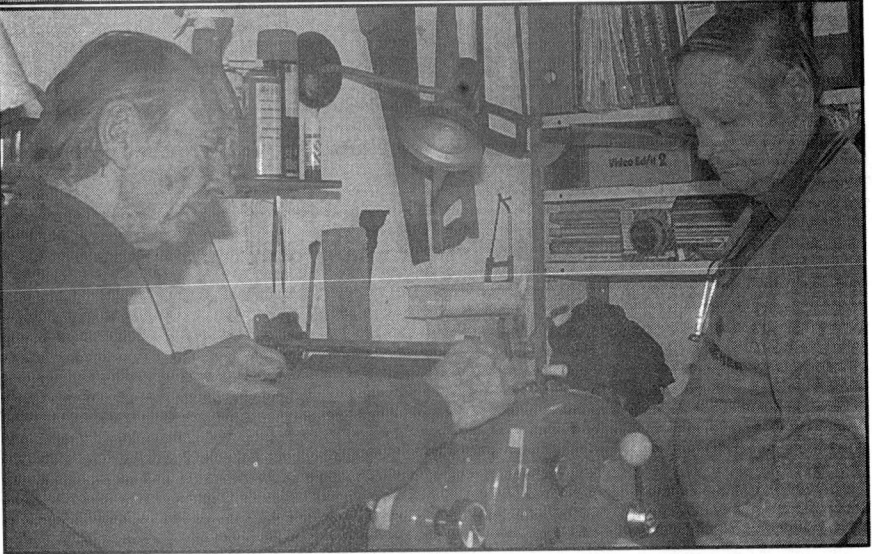

...and, so to bed!